Project Management Institute

MW00700032

Practice Standard for Project Configuration Management

Practice Standard for Project Configuration Management
ISBN 13: 978-1-930699-47-2
ISBN 10: 1-930699-47-6

Published by: Project Management Institute, Inc.
Four Campus Boulevard
Newtown Square, Pennsylvania 19073-3299 USA.
Phone: +610-356-4600
Fax: +610-356-4647
E-mail: pmihq@pmi.org
Internet: www.pmi.org

10   9   8   7   6   5   4   3   2   1

NOTICE

The Project Management Institute, Inc. (PMI) standards and guideline publications, of which the document contained herein is one, are developed through a voluntary consensus standards development process. This process brings together volunteers and/or seeks out the views of persons who have an interest in the topic covered by this publication. While PMI administers the process and establishes rules to promote fairness in the development of consensus, it does not write the document and it does not independently test, evaluate, or verify the accuracy or completeness of any information or the soundness of any judgments contained in its standards and guideline publications.

PMI disclaims liability for any personal injury, property or other damages of any nature whatsoever, whether special, indirect, consequential or compensatory, directly or indirectly resulting from the publication, use of application, or reliance on this document. PMI disclaims and makes no guaranty or warranty, expressed or implied, as to the accuracy or completeness of any information published herein, and disclaims and makes no warranty that the information in this document will fulfill any of your particular purposes or needs. PMI does not undertake to guarantee the performance of any individual manufacturer or seller's products or services by virtue of this standard or guide.

In publishing and making this document available, PMI is not undertaking to render professional or other services for or on behalf of any person or entity, nor is PMI undertaking to perform any duty owed by any person or entity to someone else. Anyone using this document should rely on his or her own independent judgment or, as appropriate, seek the advice of a competent professional in determining the exercise of reasonable care in any given circumstances. Information and other standards on the topic covered by this publication may be available from other sources, which the user may wish to consult for additional views or information not covered by this publication.

PMI has no power, nor does it undertake to police or enforce compliance with the contents of this document. PMI does not certify, test, or inspect products, designs, or installations for safety or health purposes. Any certification or other statement of compliance with any health or safety-related information in this document shall not be attributable to PMI and is solely the responsibility of the certifier or maker of the statement.

Contents

List of Table and Figures

Preface

This Project Management Institute (PMI) *Practice Standard on Project Configuration Management (PSPCM)* adds to PMI's continuing commitment to support the project management profession with a defined body of knowledge and standards.

PMI's A Guide to the Project Management Body of Knowledge (Third Edition) (*PMBOK® Guide*) documents some of the overall project management body of knowledge. Th*e PMBOK® Guide*–Third Edition is approved as an American National Standard by the American National Standards Institute,[1] and is the leading international standard for project management. This document is an extension and elaboration of the sections of the *PMBOK® Guide*–Third Edition that defines the processes, techniques, and tools used in project configuration management (PCM).[2]

This standard is a guide and reference for the project manager, team and other stakeholders, for understanding PCM and applying it appropriately in a project. Effective project management requires consistent and repeatable processes and methodologies to manage the constraints of scope, time, cost, and quality and to ensure project success. The project management professional applies configuration management to actively guide the project's direction and create a project infrastructure that enables successful completion. This standard acknowledges PCM as a supporting discipline to the project processes during the project lifecycle.

The *PSPCM* is organized into the following focus areas:

- **Introduction.** Provides the basis for the development of this standard and how it may be used by the project manager.
- **Configuration Management and Planning.** Introduces PCM concepts and their relationship to project management.
- **Configuration Identification.** Identifies project items that may be under control of PCM and provides guidance on identifying and structuring the information.
- **Configuration Change Management.** Provides guidelines in order to identify change within a project.
- **Configuration Status Accounting and Metrics.** Gives examples of the tools and techniques that can be employed to objectively measure progress and maturity of the items subject to PCM.
- **Configuration Verification and Audits.** Describes how independent scrutiny can assist a project team to confirm that the work done was the work intended.

---

[1]The American National Standards Institute is a not-for-profit organization that provides standards development guidelines.

[2]Project Management Institute. 2004. *A Guide to the Project Management Body of Knowledge (PMBOK® Guide)*–Third Edition. Newtown Square, PA.: Project Management Institute, p. 49.

Chapter 1

Introduction

Project Configuration Management (PCM) is the collective body of processes, activities, tools, and methods used to manage certain items during the project life cycle. These items are normally referred to as Configuration Items (CIs). Configuration management (CM) typically describes the mechanisms for managing the physical state of these items during their life cycle. As with any other profession, this body of knowledge rests with the practitioners who apply and advance it.

The *Practice Standard on Project Configuration Management (PSPCM)* is consistent with *A Guide to the Project Management Body of Knowledge (PMBOK® Guide)*–Third Edition, and provides additional information on the practice of PCM. The PSPCM spans all control functions found in Section 3 of the *PMBOK® Guide*–Third Edition, including the Integrated Change Control found in Chapter 4. The PSPCM describes the fundamentals of CM for practitioners of project management.

Objectives include:
- Explaining the concepts and benefits of CM in the context of project management
- Describing the types of processes used to apply CM as a project management tool
- Presenting good practices in CM in the context of project management
- Promoting a common lexicon for applying CM across projects.

This chapter defines and explains several terms, provides an overview of this standard, and includes the following major sections:

1.1 Relationship with Other Standards

The *PSPCM* provides guidelines that are relevant to project managers and project teams on the requirements and responsibilities of a sound CM system for their project. The *PSPCM* is aligned with other PMI®, national, and international standards, as well as other common practices within the field of project management.

The following are examples of existing configuration management standards:

- ASME Y14.35M–1997 (R2003) Revision of Engineering Drawings and Associated Documents
- EIA/IEEE 649 National Consensus Standard for Configuration Management
- IEEE 1042-1987 (R1993) Guide to Software Configuration Management
- ISO 10007 Quality management systems—Guidelines for configuration management

The ASME and IEEE standards provide detailed guidance for specific disciplines and types of items. Many projects have CM requirements that are not described in such discipline-oriented standards. The EIA/IEEE 649 information is very detailed and prescriptive and may provide too much detail to be readily useful to a project manager. The guidelines in ISO 10007 provide very general and high-level information useful in understanding basic CM concepts. However, it does not provide a project manager with an understanding of the impact that CM can have on a project.

The *PSPCM* provides perspectives and insights applicable to all types of projects. Managing change is a regular responsibility for project management practitioners. Controlling change is the process of configuration control. CM is the parent of configuration control. The *PSPCM* provides guidance to the project manager and project team for establishing (or ensuring the establishment of) a sound CM process for the life of a project. This practice standard provides the what, when, and why of CM for implementation on projects.

1.2 Purpose of this Practice Standard

This standard provides guidance as to the most appropriate processes and tools in a well-designed configuration management system, thereby allowing the project, program, and portfolio managers to determine if appropriate controls are in place.

This standard is written for a wide audience that includes program managers, portfolio managers, project managers, project team members, and project stakeholders. PCM is generally recognized as a good practice for projects that are technical and non-technical, minor and major, foreign and domestic, and for projects within any industry.

1.3 How to Use this Practice Standard

This practice standard is intended to provide guidance on the processes and tools related to PCM. As a foundational reference, this standard is neither comprehensive nor all-inclusive, and may be used at the discretion of the project management team. This practice standard identifies and describes a subset of CM that is generally recognized as good practice for projects, and that is applicable to most projects most of the time. Readers should therefore use discretion in applying the information contained within this document to any specific project or situation. Appendices E, F, and G provide additional tools and information, including sources of further information regarding CM.

1.4 What this Practice Standard Is Not

This practice standard is not a textbook, regulation, or legal document. It is not industry-specific nor is it a how-to guide for CM.

1.5 Why Apply PCM?

Effective project management requires consistent and repeatable processes (or methodologies) to manage the constraints of scope, time, cost, and quality, and to ensure project success. The project management professional applies CM to actively support the project's direction and infrastructure.

CM, applied over the life cycle of a configuration item, provides visibility and control of its performance, functional, and physical attributes. CM supports the following aspects of all configuration items (CIs) contained in any system:

- Integrity;
- Accountability;
- Visibility;
- Reproducibility;
- Coordination;
- Formal controllability; and
- Traceability.

To accomplish the preceding attributes, PCM *may* utilize consistent and reusable tools.

Within the processes of project planning, execution, and control, CM is critical. Figure 1-1 illustrates a failure mode and effect analysis (FMEA) that supports the use of PCM.

When PCM techniques are applied, many benefits are gained, including:

- Maintaining the integrity of CIs;
- Communication interfaces are clearer and contain applicable information;
- Records are available to support project or customer auditing requirements;
- Historical information regarding deliverable CIs can be utilized through the deliverable life;
- Integration between planning, execution, and change control help keep requirements and the end results of the project synchronized; and
- Ensuring only approved changes are incorporated into a revised configuration item.

Project Configuration Management

Failure Mode	Effect	Cause	Proposed Control
Project deliverables and working papers fail to align, conflict with each other, impact/overlay each other, or are used inappropriately.	Project fails to meet requirements, commitments, or expectations of stakeholders.	Inconsistent or incorrect configuration management of project resources and work products.	Develop and deploy a new configuration management standard that is suitable for the needs of the projects.

Areas of Concern

- Product domains within projects often have PCM for domain-specific items (e.g., software, engineering diagrams, formulas).
- Project managers need PCM for process specific items (e.g., plans, contracts, agreements, assignments, status reports, dashboards, scorecards).
- Cross discipline artifacts (i.e., those possibly thought of as either project management items *and* domain-specific items such as requirements) present special problems because they are possibly subject to PCM in *both* domain-specific and project methods.

Figure 1-1. FMEA Justification for PCM

1.6 Key Points

Some of the key points addressed within this practice standard are listed in this section. They are discussed within this practice standard and help clarify the depth of PCM.

CM planning often goes beyond the bounds of the project to ensure coordination of the project with its surrounding environment and to ensure integration of the project into a larger application if necessary. These external considerations should be documented as part of the project requirements in the earliest stages of a project to ensure that project integration is addressed, planned, and documented.

PCM requires human and system interfaces with other project processes to ensure that plans and priorities of CM align with those of the overall project plan. Clearly defined project interfaces for ensuring effective and efficient communications among the project stakeholders, suppliers, customers, and systems are needed for integration of CM requirements and compliance.

PCM provides a proactive perspective to the interdependent project management processes of initiating, planning, executing, controlling, and closing. This perspective addresses the planning for changes within all the project management processes as far in advance as possible.

CM is a well-established practice in many disciplines. However, projects are often cross-disciplinary endeavors, and specific disciplines often have their own configuration management strategies and procedures. A challenge for the project manager is to plan and execute PCM on project CIs while harmonizing with the CM needs and capabilities of all of the disciplines engaged in the project.

Controlling changes to approved project baselines is a fundamental PCM function. Early in planning, the project team should determine the project items requiring CM and the processes for managing them.

Some projects may be required to maintain configuration information under very strict controls mandated by a government or industry regulation. In these cases, external circumstances or organizational policies establish the processes and policies that the project will follow. These processes and policies are described in project plans, specifically in the documentation describing the change control system.

PCM ensures audit reports, summaries, checklists, action item status, deliverables, and other related documentation are retained and available in a timely and informative manner for stakeholders, project managers, and senior management to review at any point in time to determine the project's health.

1.7 Audience

This practice standard provides a basic reference for anyone interested in PCM. This includes:
- Senior executives;
- Project managers;
- Project team members; and
- Stakeholders
- Consultants in the field of project management.

For CM practitioners, the sole intention of this practice standard is to provide an understanding of how their processes may impact the project.

Chapter 2

Configuration Management Planning

As with all planning processes described in the *PMBOK® Guide*–Third Edition, the Configuration Management (CM) Planning Process plans all aspects of PCM. This chapter describes considerations for planning and managing PCM. It explains the context of PCM and the relationship with good CM practices. It also highlights how vital communication of PCM is and provides descriptions of the human and system interfaces for CM. It includes the following major sections:

2.1   **Overview**
2.2   **Organization**
2.3   **Communications**
2.4   **Training**
2.5   **CM and PCM**

2.1 Overview

The *PMBOK® Guide*–Third Edition identifies tools which are used to successfully accomplish a project. The tools (such as the project charter, project baseline, and project change control log) provide a basis for, and a record of, the project's performance in meeting the scope, time, cost, and quality. They identify and provide for impact assessment of changes to the planned scope, schedule, and budget as the project progresses. The tools promote communications to ensure that the project outcome meets stakeholders' needs.

CM is a discipline that helps ensure that the post-project functionality is planned and documented. PCM requirements vary by project from minimal efforts to the prime purpose of a project. For example:

- An increase to the authorized speed limit on a local highway requires a project to replace ten speed-limit sign faces. The CM effort may be limited to identifying the sign faces that require replacement and updating the sign inventory to reflect the change.
- The owner of a new car wash requires a project to build the facility. The CM effort may include developing a master equipment list identifying each physical component in the facility (including parts identification, approved suppliers, main-

tenance requirements and schedules, and maintenance history), as well as managing the development of the facility.

- Changes in consumer eating-habits require a project to develop a new capability to constantly allocate/reallocate the shelf, refrigerator, and freezer space. The CM effort may include planning for and providing automated tracking systems that integrate and optimize product sales and inventory with available space to showcase the product.

Figure 2-1 illustrates relationships among project and deliverable configuration items (CIs).

For a self-contained project with no clients (i.e., contributors or users of the application and deliverables or items resulting from the project), CM may be a subset of the project management plan.

2.2 Organization

A project is generally organized with a project sponsor acting as the single point-of-contact for the project's stakeholders. The project sponsor typically delegates requirements for the required level of CM to the project team through the project manager. The project manager is, therefore, responsible for coordinating the efforts of the project team to ensure that the project approach to CM is aligned with the requirements and expectations of the stakeholders. This is a consideration because the output of a project can be an interface or an input to the stakeholders' own configuration process or system. Note that the stakeholders can have their own CM processes and systems.

For small or simple projects where minimal coordination or planning is required, the project manager may also act as the configuration manager. On large or complex projects, a separate configuration manager may be appointed to interface between the project team and the individual application stakeholders.

At the project level, PCM issues are addressed in a PCM plan. The PCM plan could include:

- Authorities, roles, responsibilities, and disciplines involved;
- Identification of controlled items (i.e., configuration items (CI));
- Configuration control processes and procedures;
- Status accounting and metric definitions; and
- List of PCM audits and procedures as well as their relationships to project schedules.

Figure 2-2 illustrates typical interfaces required to address PCM and CM Interface.

Overlap of Project and Product Domain Items

Project Items	Overlapping Items	Application Items
• Schedule	• CM Plan	• Maintenance Records
• Project Plans	• Master Equipment List	• Software Code
• Issue Logs	• Spare Parts List	• Technical Manuals
• Risk Assessments	• Procurement Control	• Procurement Records
• Status Reports	• Modification Records	• Drawings
• Scope Items	• Accountable Documents	

Project Domain   **Product Domain**

Figure 2-1. Overlap of Project and Deliverable Configuration Items

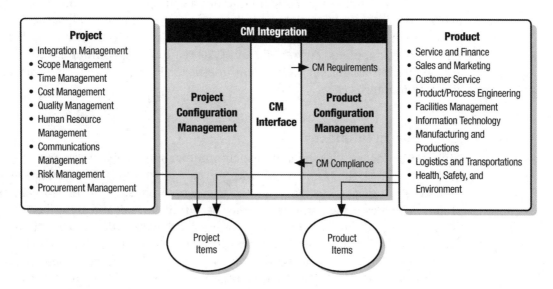

Figure 2-2. PCM and CM Interface

2.3 Communications

Sound, fundamental, quality communications are fundamental for the integration of PCM activities into the project management plan. Communication is also a key process for the management of PCM points of interaction. Good interface management is essential for the systematic communication of PCM information and control of the points of interaction.

Figure 2-3 illustrates a simple PCM communications system and the flow of PCM change information for a project. The arrows show the flows of information.

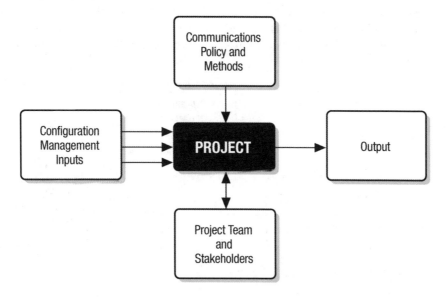

Figure 2-3. PCM Communications

PCM requires human and system interfaces with other project processes to ensure plans and priorities of CM align with those of the overall project plan. Clearly defined project interfaces provide effective and efficient communications among the project stakeholders, suppliers, customers, and systems. In PCM, communication interfaces are categorized as human and system interfaces. Figure 2-4 depicts project human and system interfaces.

2.3.1 Human Interfaces

Human interfaces cover the complex communications between people or groups of people. For PCM, the human interfaces are categorized as internal or external.

Internal interfaces are those among the people engaged on the project and the project activities. These interfaces may be either formal and described in project documents or informal where project members proactively develop solutions through communication of information. Informal interfaces, as a minimum, should be followed up with communication of the discussion to verify that there is indeed agreement with the conclusions of the discussion and to ensure a history of the discussion is documented. The informal interfaces develop as project members learn how to avert and solve problems through communication of information.

The external interfaces involve communication among the project team and persons outside the team. Such interfaces can be with stakeholders, suppliers, and supporting organizations. Other external interfaces may be the end users impacted by the change related to the defined PCM. Defining external interfaces provides a means for communication methods and channels to integrate the external end-users within the change process.

2.3.2 System Interfaces

System interfaces are the artifacts created to share data between systems and between systems and humans. System interfaces are defined by processes and are described in formal documents such as the project scope management plan. System interfaces also deal with establishing processes and structures that ensure compliance with regulations and standards. In most projects, system interfaces concern the various application-specific CM standards and processes related to practice disciplines.

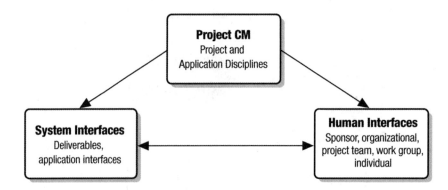

Figure 2-4. System and Human Interfaces

2.4 Training

In some cases, complex projects require formal training for the project stakeholders to understand the need, requirement, development, and maintenance of a PCM plan and related activities.

2.5 Configuration Management and PCM

Projects are often cross-disciplinary endeavors. Specific disciplines will often have their own CM strategies and procedures. A challenge for the project manager is to plan and execute CM on project CIs while harmonizing with the CM needs and capabilities of all the disciplines engaged in the project. The term "harmonization" is used to describe a condition where the configuration management systems of a project manage unique CIs; do not conflict in practice, schedule, or resource usage; and share lexicon and vocabulary needed for effective interface communications among stakeholders. Figure 2-5 describes the harmonization concepts.

Figure 2-6 expands on the concept of harmonizing multiple approaches to PCM on a project involving several disciplines. Figure 2-6 also shows some of the considerations in assuring that PCM and discipline CM work together on a project.

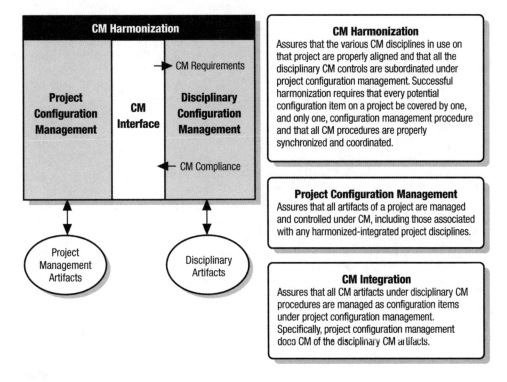

Figure 2-5. Harmonization of Project and Discipline CM

Project CM and Discipline CM

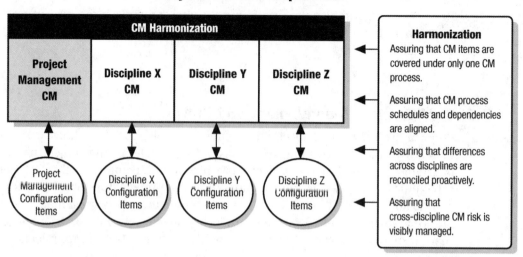

Figure 2-6. PCM and Discipline CM

Chapter 3

Configuration Identification

Throughout the life of a project, information is needed to help direct and manage the project. Creating, modifying, and storing this information is an important part of the project. This chapter describes what to identify on the project that may be placed under PCM control. The chapter begins by describing what to look for in identifying project information and items that may be under the control of the PCM process. It also provides guidance in structuring the information so that it is more accessible to those who need it. Part of the structuring involves determining what items need to have an assigned identifier and then giving them a unique identification to allow them to be managed as configuration items (CIs).

This chapter includes the following major sections:

3.1 **Project Artifacts**
3.2 **Structure**
3.3 **Item Identification**
3.4 **Taxonomy Scheme**

3.1 Project Artifacts

From the very beginning of a project, documents and other artifacts are created that help manage the project and provide communications to the project team, stakeholders, management, and others. Some documents and other artifacts describe the project itself and its various characteristics. For instance, the project charter lays out what the project is intended to accomplish and requirements definition identifies the expected capabilities of the final project deliverable. Other information explains the agreed upon relationship between the various organizations that are either a part of the project or that support it. Included here might be contracts with vendors, subcontractors, and suppliers, as well as agreements for support with other groups within the same organization.

The following list has many examples of information that could be under the control of PCM:

Change information	Organizational breakdown	Risk register
Contracts	structure	Schedule information
Cost artifacts	Planning documents	Statement of work
Invitation for bid	Project management plan	Work breakdown structure
Metrics	Quality plan	

This list should not be considered as required information for every project. It is provided simply to illustrate possible documents for a variety of projects. The actual collection varies from one project to another, and in all likelihood includes only a few of these items, as well as additional items that are specific to a particular project or organizational policy.

3.2 Structure

As with any important collection of information, a method of structuring project documents and artifacts under PCM is needed. The most basic structuring requirement is for a filing system that makes it possible to organize the information for efficient storage, retrieval, and use. It may also address other project needs, including:

- **Information Format.** Project information may exist in two forms: electronic and hard copy; and both need to be structured appropriately for the project. Although the methods used differ, the objective is the same: making it possible to efficiently manage project documents and artifacts with the right balance of accessibility, storage indexing, security, and recoverability.
- **Rapid Access.** It is important that information frequently used by the project manager and core project team is easily accessible. To facilitate this, some project managers create what they call a project binder (may be either electronic or hard copy.) This binder contains such items as project and staffing plans, contact information, various reports, budget information, and other reference information.
- **Broad Availability.** It is also important for information used by several members of the project team to be kept in an easily accessible location. A typical method is to have the information in computer-based files with secure network access. Computer-based files permit all members of the team access to the same, current information quickly from any location having computer access, including over the Internet. This is particularly important for a project whose team is geographically dispersed. Care should be used in administering the controls for adding, updating, or deleting the information to ensure that only authorized changes are permitted and that these are made to the correct version of the artifact.
- **Secure Access.** Some information may be sensitive. For such information, proper access controls can be used to limit access to only those people who have a need to view or change the information. Personnel and budgeting information as well as some correspondence requires special treatment to safeguard personnel and organizational information. Properly implemented access controls can also help ensure data and information integrity.
- **Information Recovery.** A plan for recovering any project document or artifact that is lost or otherwise made inaccessible is another important element of the information storage plan. A recovery plan defines how the project artifacts are backed up, when and how frequently, and the recovery process for specific items. An example of a specific item is the recovery of an older version.
- **Information Retention.** Occasionally, situations arise where older information that has been replaced with more current information needs to be referenced. A plan for archiving older versions of information for future reference may be useful on some projects.

For many projects, particularly larger ones, where a lot of project documentation is expected to be produced, it may be beneficial to have a well thought out documentation plan. A documentation plan lays out the details about how the project documentation is to be structured and managed, and it is usually developed early in the project cycle. The plan may identify storage locations for the information described earlier in this document. For documents that will be undergoing revisions, the plan may also describe the progression for document versions from inception to use and from update to eventual archival. It may also note any applicable changes in storage locations as a document progresses from one state to another. The documentation plan may be easily accessible to the project team as well as anyone who is responsible for filing new or changed documents. Access however should be in accordance with the security and privacy policies of the organization. Once created, the documentation plan would be placed under PCM.

3.3 Item Identification

Configuration identification is an organized structure describing the composition of objects within a project. These objects are termed CIs. Standard baseline descriptions of the functional and physical attributes of these CIs are established to maintain control of changes occurring to existing items and new "end items" or deliverables within projects.

Generally, the project processes result in establishing approved baselines and related descriptions in a timely manner. Any changes from the baselines are documented for their effect on unique items and are approved. The baselines reflect the differences from the "as planned" through to the "as released."

Identification of configuration items emphasizes the final deliverables of the project as well as significant events or effects, and presents both the manager and client or sponsor with recognizable points of achievement. Items selected from the project are at a level significant enough to maintain control and may consist of (1) physical items, (2) documents, (3) forms, and (4) records. These four categories can be subdivided by type and baseline. Examples of significant items are:

- Items that must meet legal requirements;
- Items that must meet health and safety guidelines;
- Items to be sent out to subcontractors;
- Items that have an impact on processes or deliverables outside of the current project; and
- Items that form a large component of the project's deliverable.

3.4 Taxonomy Scheme

Formal review processes, status tracking, and management of changes require that information describing one CI be differentiated from information describing other CIs. In practice, projects have found that CIs must be uniquely identified for control, processing, and tracking. Unique identification can be accomplished by assigning serial numbers, non-significant numbers or any established and project-approved classification to each CI.

Language usage within an identifier has been shown to reduce identification errors and to allow ease of use. Therefore, the trend is to use a mix of meaningful letters (e.g., denoting type of CI and numbers (such as date, version, etc). Some organizations have identifiers in place for use in all activities.

The complexity and sophistication needed for a cataloging system reflects the project's size and relationships. The more complex the system is, the more time, resources, and budget should be assigned to the CI portion and taxonomy schemes.

Depending on the type of project and corporate policies, the following identifier types can be considered:

- Intelligent identifier referencing specifics by including within the ID code;
  - Category of item (i.e., physical, document, form, record);
  - Hierarchical association to other items (blueprints, systems specifications); and
  - Version control (original, upgrade, complete change, subcontractor/manufacturer, plant location);
- Date stamp;
- Source of the item (project, subcontract, existing company item);
- Format (if computer based, then word-processing software, version, and platform); and
- Serialization or lot control.

Chapter 4

Configuration Change Management

This chapter provides information about managing change in the context of PCM. It expands upon information presented in the *PMBOK® Guide*–Third Edition and provides specific guidance with respect to the processes used for managing change on a project. It includes the following major sections:

4.1 Overview
4.2 Identification
4.3 Process
4.4 Control
4.5 Assessment and Approval
4.6 Implementation
4.7 Verification and Acceptance
4.8 Closure

4.1 Overview

The *PMBOK® Guide*– Third Edition defines Configuration Management (CM) as a subsystem of overall project management. The processes in PCM are utilized when managing the fundamental project constraints of scope, time, cost, and quality. Configuration Change Management (CCM) plays a crucial role in managing these constraints, as it encompasses the processes and procedures used to administer changes to Configuration Items (CIs).

Applying CCM principles to project artifacts ensures a number of benefits including:
- The correct version of the configuration item is in use by the project team;
- Changes to configuration items are made only by authorized individuals;
- A planned means of notifying stakeholders of approved changes to configuration items is in place; and
- A record of configuration item changes is kept to support auditing and project closure activities.

CCM is applied when identifying and documenting changes and their impact on configuration items. Changes are then processed through the project's change control system. In many application areas, the change control system is a subset of the configuration management system, as described in Figure 4-1.

Figure 4-2 illustrates the process required to execute configuration change management.

The individual phases of the configuration change management process are described as follows:

- **Baseline:** This is the latest baseline released by CM.
- **Submit Change Request:** This step prepares the request, ensuring that adequate information is supplied to allow proper assessment of the impact of the change.
- **Verify Change Request:** This step ensures that all the information needed to carry out an evaluation has been provided. It establishes relationships between the proposed changes and the items that will be impacted by the change.
- **Evaluate Impacts:** This step evaluates the impact of the proposed change. Technical, cost, schedule, security, and contract impacts are all evaluated. Identifying the appropriate people to carry out the evaluation may be challenging. The need to ensure that all impacts are identified must be balanced with the need to executing the process efficiently by doing only the necessary evaluations.
- **Review Decision and Plan:** This step considers the proposed change in light of the evaluated impact. The authority required to approve a change will vary according to the type and status of items affected. A proposed change may, of course, be rejected. Items which actually need to be changed are confirmed and work packages are established and/or adjusted.
- **Implement Change if Approved:** This step makes the change, tracks the progress, and reports status to the tracking system. Relationships between the change record and the item(s) actually affected by the change are established and updated.
- **Conclude Change Process:** This step ensures that the CCM process has been correctly followed and that there is appropriate evidence that changes have been satisfactorily implemented (typically a review process for documents, testing for code). Authority to conclude a change is the same as the authority to prove it. Status is reported to the tracking system.

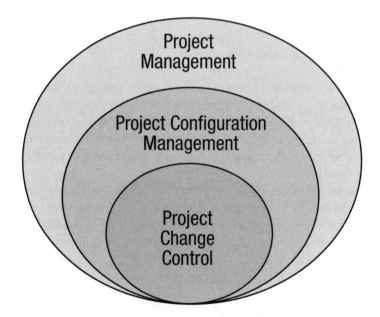

Figure 4-1. The Hierarchy of Control Mechanisms Involving CCM

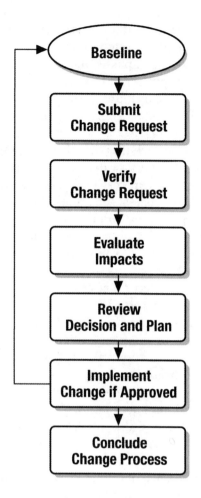

Figure 4-2. CCM Process.

4.2 Identification

The *PMBOK® Guide*–Third Edition suggests that a clear distinction be made between plans and project performance measurement baselines. Specifically, it defines plans as project deliverables that should be expected to change over time and states that performance measurement baselines change only in response to approved scope of work or deliverable changes.

The identification of project deliverables as CIs may be either formal or informal. The level of formality, the complexity of the CCM process, and the cost of supporting the procedures should be appropriate to the needs of the project.

CCM is usually described in the project change control plan or in a separate CM plan if project size and complexity justify it. Ideally, the CCM process is described in one document and scalable to the project. Ultimately, CCM should be readily visible to project stakeholders so that constraints (scope, time, cost, and quality) can be managed successfully.

4.3 Process

The change management process describes integrated change control as a system that covers the creation and value assessment of change requests. In addition, the change management process includes maintenance of baselines and managing the approved changes. In some systems, authorization for making changes or document modifications is tracked and in other systems authorization is electronically controlled through security access. CCM encompasses the processes used to administer change to CIs. A project may have a number of change management processes.

CCM may be governed by industry standards or practice. CCM systems and components have been developed for some practices, such as manufacturing, software development, and construction.

A CCM process may include a number of components and a structured process flow. The structured process flow describes the activities, inputs, outputs, and controls for each step of a change process life cycle. The CCM components are mechanisms that support the CCM process. A database listing information about CIs is one such component. A change request form is another.

A CCM process has processes and procedures that serve to assure that all necessary aspects of configuration change management are addressed and decisions are accurately reflected. The CCM process serves a number of purposes in addition to prescribing administrative procedures. For example, the process helps ensure:

- Stakeholders' viewpoints are addressed;
- Impacts on scope, time, cost, and quality are identified and documented;
- Assigned personnel conduct evaluations;
- Recommendations and approvals are sought and recorded; and
- Decisions are communicated by means of appropriate internal and external human interfaces.

It is important to remember that the CCM process requires that the related procedures are documented and that the appropriate configuration baselines are established. It is imperative that the baselines provide for the identification and control of the CIs.

In general, the sequence of events for an iteration of the CCM process begins with the determination that a change is required. The impetus for change, for example, can be an improvement, a new requirement, clarification of an existing requirement, or an externally mandated change. The project documentation establishes responsibilities and procedures for documenting the need for change, as well as procedures for submitting a change request. Note that the change control process has the tools and techniques needed for the submission, recording, and retention of change requests.

The CCM process is a type of workflow, where the first set of activities involves the recognition and documentation of a needed change and the entry of that information into the change management system.

The next set of activities is concerned with the evaluation and approval of the change request. These activities and their sequence can be quite complex if several organizations and/or a large body of documentation is involved. Often, the evaluation includes review by a Configuration or Change Control Board (CCB) or equivalent.

The next set of activities includes those related to processing the results of the evaluation and approval activities. These activities include providing notifications, preparing for implementation of approved changes, implementing the changes, and validating that the changes occurred. Note that in some projects, the verification of change is performed by an operating element and a separate organizational element subsequently verifies the implementation.

4.4 Control

Fundamental control of changes to configuration items (CIs) may be achieved through a Project Management Information System (PMIS), which supports a full audit trail and reporting of change requests. The requests contain information appropriate to managing changes to project deliverables. Depending on the application area and on the degree of deliverable complexity, the PMIS may be augmented or supplemented by a CI database.

Formal controls of CIs tend to focus on the unique deliverable being produced. Application areas such as architecture, engineering, construction, manufacturing, and computer systems frequently are governed by industry standards or formal practice guidelines.

Whether formal or informal, change management control ensures that each change request is tracked over its lifetime. Tracking would normally include the following as a minimum: unique tracking number, originator information, time stamp, and synopsis of request.

4.5 Assessment and Approval

The project manager bears ultimate responsibility for the integrity of the change request process, and for tracking work on the implementation of the approved change request resolution. Responsibility for approvals and rejection of a change request is established in the project process documents. This responsibility may be assigned to a qualified technical stakeholder at any level in the hierarchy.

A project charter or other requirements may impose change control information requirements on a project. This can be expected when a project is part of a program of related projects. Points of contact hierarchies are more complex for programs than for projects. The level of effort for program CCM is expected to be greater than for project CCM.

If a contract applies, legal and client stakeholders should be included in the point of contact hierarchy. This may be expected to increase the level of effort. These stakeholders may have change request rejection authority, depending on the nature of the contract and the level of risk exposure and risk tolerance.

4.6 Implementation

Some basic requirements to implement change on a CI are:
- Documented approval;
- Use of CM tools and techniques appropriate to the application area; and
- Documentation of relevant quality metrics and testing results appropriate to the application area.

4.7 Verification and Acceptance

Verification and acceptance of a change request resolution is achieved only after the authorization of an appropriate business or technical stakeholder is obtained. In some cases, formal testing or regulatory approval is required before a change can be accepted. Verification and acceptance ensures that only authorized changes are implemented.

4.8 Closure

The authority of an appropriate business or technical stakeholder, acknowledging successful implementation of an approved change request resolution within relevant scope, time, cost, and quality bounds, is both necessary and sufficient for change request closure. A deliverable should not be considered complete until all change requests impacting that deliverable are closed.

Chapter 5

Configuration Status Accounting and Metrics

This chapter describes maintaining and reporting information about the CM items and related actions, such as pending changes. A project may use configuration status and accounting to disseminate information, validate and verify actions, and to serve as the feedback mechanism for the overall PCM process. This chapter includes the following major sections:

    5.1   **Information Repository**
    5.2   **Reporting**
    5.3   **Analysis**

5.1 Information Repository

Chapter 2 provided repository examples used in PCM and CM, and Chapter 3 provided examples mentioned in the *PMBOK® Guide*–Third Edition. Information repositories are essential to PCM. An information repository is a place (database, library, or file system) where project information is deposited for controlled storage, access, version, and version control. A project may have one or many repositories. The PCM plan could describe the repositories and the processes for their use. The PCM plan could also show the relationships and any interfaces among these repositories, their processes, and the people who use them. Configuration status accounting (CSA) involves acquiring and entering information into the applicable repository. For inputting and later locating information, it has been found useful for the repository to be organized systematically. WBS, OBS, or document hierarchies are examples of ways to organize the repository's structure.

Based on the information gathered, a series of metrics are developed for analysis. Configuration status accounting (CSA) provides the data necessary to validate if approved changes have been consistent with the project's objectives and can be traced to the project scope and its evolution. This data repository includes various benchmark, baseline, and production level metrics, in conjunction with the revision level history for all hardware, software, and documentation.

5.2 Reporting

CSA and metrics reporting produces management information for the project. This information can be used to baseline a production level metric, control changes to this metric, and track any improvement the metric provides the project over time. Once a baseline production level metric has been established, periodic tracking reports can be produced on CM activities, project quality, and measured performance over time.

5.2.1 Status

Status in the PCM context requires that PCM has control over all CIs, can show an audit trail and the artifacts of all changes including all versions of the CIs, and show the status of each version. Status of a change to the CI should indicate its stage in the life cycle, such as draft, in review, approved, not effective, effective, retired, or obsolete. Status also indicates whether changes are pending to a CI. The level of detail and control is related to risk, regulations, and standards. For example, it is expected that more resources will be expended on maintaining strict controls and records about scope than on the minutes of weekly project team meetings.

Status accounting tracks the status of approved changes. As such, PCM status accounting serves as a control mechanism to inform the project manager about the results of an approved change. The status of each CI is determined in agreement with CCM processes. Coordination and communication are essential to ensure that the changes that are planned and the data to be tracked within a given change are identified well in advance. A collection plan, even if it is as simple as a checklist, helps to ensure the necessary data is captured. Necessary data may include which CIs are addressed in given technical and verification reviews, so that the required status information is provided on time according to the project plan. Another possible status request may be to report the number of change requests submitted, and of these submissions, how many were rejected and why.

5.2.2 Metrics

Metrics are a communication tool used by the project manager to assess control of the project and determine if process improvements are needed.

Metrics track what was changed, when it was changed, and what impact, if any, the change had on the previously captured data and potential effects on new data. These records should include enough detail to allow analysis and investigation of processes that may become unstable after a change was made. The optimum set of metrics and their scale of granularity depend on the organization strategies, resources, technologies, and business sectors. Some metrics may be measured in time scale or tolerances and others in cost. Each measurement can help the project meet the needs of its stakeholders.

Metrics help to estimate the effort required for CIs by establishing benchmarks for previous similar work efforts. These estimates of effort may help the project manager to identify trends in the productivity of implementing various CIs, determine if estimating techniques are valid, track customer satisfaction, and track rework. They can help to determine the impact a proposed change might have, and this may in turn aid decision making. This data may also help to facilitate the communication across the project, since decision-making data could be readily accessible by all.

For maximum utility, data may be presented to the project manager in a suitable format for enhanced analysis. This formatting may include numerical values, graphical representation, tables, or text.

5.2.3 Benchmarking

Project benchmarking involves comparing project processes, tools, and techniques with other projects. The other projects can be within or outside the project-owning organization. The Project Management Institute's *Organizational Project Management Maturity Model (OPM3®)* is a source of best practices that can be used for comparison and measurement. Benchmarks are useful in planning PCM and in analyzing results.

Benchmarking is the process of capturing data from a functioning system. This data could be from a test system before it encounters any load, or it could be captured from a similar production system that a new application intends to surpass. PCM may also require a more specific type of benchmarking. Benchmarking can be prepared for any aspect of a system including: training time, learning curve, ease of use, as well as the normal data items of response time, customer serve time, and end-user satisfaction. For PCM, this type of benchmarking produces configuration items that are multipurpose. These items feed into the quality assurance processes and may trigger requests for changes such as corrective action based on variance analyses.

5.2.4 Performance Measures

Performance measures vary greatly depending on the type of application being developed. These measures can be expressed as Key Performance Indicators (KPIs) such as:
- **Quantitative**. This measure requires the definition of a set of objective metric(s) which can be expressed as a specific quantity such as an amount, sum, or number.
- **Qualitative**. This measure requires the definition of a project-specific set of non-computational attributes or characteristics.

5.2.5 Delivering Operational Statistics

Operational statistics can include Statistical Process Control (SPC) artifacts. Examples include control charts, run charts, feedback from users and customers, and overall determination as to whether the change met the desired result.

Operational statistics normally provide a measure of the repeatability and reproducibility required for determination of project stability over time. SPC can be used to measure process stability over time, and can provide a stable benchmark for auditing any data changes after change implementation.

5.2.6 Providing Reports

Status accounting provides either periodic or ad hoc reports. These reports are a communication tool that describes the change control activity and the status of the CIs. The reports may provide the following types of information:
.1 **Baselines:**
- when created and by whom;
- where the information is stored, and how to gain access to it.

.2 Change Requests:
- new since last report;
- active change requests and their status in the change process; and
- approved requests since the last report and action to implement;
- details of requests rejected

.3 Notifications:
- change notices and distribution for requested changes and the affected CIs; and
- changed CIs.

.4 Implementation Status:
- changes being implemented and their status; and
- audits planned.

5.3 Analysis

Analysis of process improvement metrics helps to determine if the project change management process is functioning as planned by improving the overall system. Trend data can be used to monitor performance levels. Measurement data variation may be related to any number of causes. Environment changes, the measuring procedure and equipment, and numerous other factors may impact the measurement data captured.

Chapter 6

Configuration Verification and Audits

The purpose of configuration verification and audit (CVA) is to ensure the composition of a project's CIs and CI changes are registered, assessed, approved, tracked, and correctly implemented.

The verification and audit process may encompass the following:

- Integrity of CI information;
- Accuracy and reproducibility of CI History;
- Traceability of the project's CIs across the project management process as well as between CIs; and
- Documentation is completed that defines the project.

PCM verification and audit establishes that the functional and performance requirements of a project and its deliverables have been achieved by the design and project implementation. PCM verification and audit is performed on initial, interim and final deliverable versions including whenever a CI is baselined or released. This chapter includes the following major sections:

    6.1   Verification
    6.2   Audit
    6.3   Verification and Audit Activities

6.1 Verification

PCM verification ensures that PCM's goals are achieved through a systematic comparison of requirements with the initial, interim and final results of testing, analysis, demonstration or inspections.

6.2 Audit

PCM audit is the independent process of ensuring the project's CIs were built according to their defined documentation. An audit is not intended to replace reviews, tests, or inspections of the project's deliverables.

PCM auditing increases the visibility of a project, compares the actual process with the documented process, and uncovers any process deficiencies. The PCM audit provides an additional tool to help a project manager determine how well a project is going, to identify and reassess risks, and to solve problems.

PCM verification is usually accomplished through formal CM audits, which are usually conducted at least once for each release, such as: Functional Configuration Audit (FCA), and Physical Configuration Audit (PCA).

Additional PCM audits may include:

- Assessing spare part quantities and configuration;
- Determining the currently installed equipment components and configuration; and
- Audit and change control results.

6.3 Verification and Audit Activities

PCM verification and audit activities consist of planning, execution, report creation and communications.

6.3.1 Planning Verification and Audits

It is essential for the PCM verification and audit to be planned at each project's critical points, where major configuration risks are most likely to occur. Some organizations have an enterprise CM plan that establishes CM policies, processes, and procedures to be used by all projects. Any existing enterprise CM plan may be adapted to a project's needs and the appropriate PCM verifications and audits scheduled.

6.3.2 Executing Verification and Audits

It is essential for a project manager to establish the necessary time, structure, and resources to do the PCM verification and audit activities as planned in the project's CM plan or project management plan. Through CM, a project manager needs to ensure all recommendations and nonconformity issues are addressed and appropriately scheduled for correction.

6.3.3 Reporting

The following identifies PCM reports that a project manager may expect from the verification and audit process:

- Reports indicating the PCM audit results and recommendation to proceed or not to proceed to the next activity or task; and
- Release notes indicating the contents of the baseline or release, known deficiencies, list of components and component versions, workarounds to provide temporary fixes, and what has changed since the last release note (including the identification of repairs), etc.

6.3.4 Communicating Results of Verification and Audits

A project manager has the responsibility to communicate the PCM verification and audit results to the appropriate stakeholders as established in the project's communications plan or CM plan.

Appendix A

Guidelines for a Project Management Institute Practice Standard

- Each practice standard provides guidelines on the mechanics (e.g., nuts and bolts, basics, fundamentals, step-by-step usage guide, how it operates, how to do it) of some significant process (input, tool, technique, or output) that is relevant to a project manager.
- A practice standard does not necessarily mirror the life-cycle phases of many projects. However, an individual practice standard may be applicable to the completion of one or more phases within a project.
- A practice standard does not necessarily mirror the knowledge areas within *A Guide to the Project Management Body of Knowledge (PMBOK® Guide*–Third Edition*)*, although an individual practice standard will provide sufficient detail and background for one or more of the inputs, tools and techniques, and/or outputs. Therefore, practice standards are not required to use the name of any Knowledge Area.
- Each practice standard should include information on *what* the significant process is and does, *why* it is significant, *when* it should be performed and, if necessary for further clarification, *who* should perform it.
- Each practice standard should include information that is accepted and applicable for most projects most of the time within the project management community. Processes that are generally restricted or applicable to one industry, country, or companion profession (i.e., an application area) may be included as an appendix for informational purposes, rather than part of the practice standard. With strong support and evidence, an application area-specific process may be considered as an *extension* of a practice standard, in the same manner as extensions to the *PMBOK® Guide*–Third Edition are considered.
- Each practice standard will benefit from the inclusion of examples and templates in the appendices. It is best when an example or template includes a discussion of its strengths and weaknesses. A background description may be necessary to place this discussion in the appropriate context. The examples and templates featured should be aligned with the relevant information that appears in the standard or other appendices.

- All practice standards will be written in the same general style and format, in accordance with PMI's preferred style manual.
- Each practice standard project will assess the need to align with or reference other practice standards.
- Each practice standard will be consistent with the current edition of the *PMBOK® Guide.*
- Each practice standard is intended to be more prescriptive than the current edition of the *PMBOK® Guide.*

Appendix B

Evolution of the Practice Standard on Project Configuration Management

This practice standard was developed from a driving need to explain in detail the interactions of the controlling processes within the *PMBOK® Guide–Third Edition*. During the development of the *PMBOK® Guide* 2000, several gaps were identified in the controlling processes throughout the document. The scope of closing those gaps as well as the explanation of how configuration management (CM) interfaced with project management was just too voluminous. This resulted in the projected changes being outside the scope of the *PMBOK® Guide*.

The next evolution was to determine the best mechanism for clarifying the issues found in the *PMBOK® Guide*. The Standards Member Advisory Group (SMAG) debated and concluded that a practice standard would be the best solution for explaining how CM plays into the project management realm.

Practitioners of the project management discipline battle every day with changes to their projects. Controlling these changes is the process of Configuration Control. Configuration management (CM) is the parent discipline to Configuration Control. The *Practice Standard on Project Configuration Management* provides guidance to the project manager and project team for establishing (or ensuring the establishment of) a sound CM process for the life of a project.

In March of 2002 the *Practice Standard on Project Configuration Management* Project was chartered. This mechanism began the process of finding volunteers and to write the first release of the standard. A Project Leadership Team (PLT) was formed with Elden F. Jones II, MSPM, PMP serving as project manager. The project was organized with a deputy project manager and managers for content, quality, configuration management, and editing. The PLT prepared operating documentation including work breakdown structure (WBS), project management plan (PMP), configuration management plan, and schedule. Initially, the PLT and volunteers conducted discussions on why another standard was being developed. Throughout the year 2003, the project documentation was refined and the process of seeking and assigning volunteers continued. The PLT developed a straw man for the standard, which the SMAG approved.

In early 2004, the content team was formed. Initially, the content team spent several weeks discussing the charter and scope of the standard. Considerable discussion centered on the differences between prescriptive and proscriptive language. The content team also discussed the value which the project configuration management standard should deliver to the reader. The team found that other PMI documentation and standards treated CM as a tool, rather than addressing "project CM." The content team agreed to present CM as a transcendent supporting process on a project. This helped develop a standard that filled the gap between the high-level CM standards such as ISO 10007 and detailed standards such as EIA 649.

The content team was organized into groups for each major portion of the straw man outline. Each group was responsible for developing content based on the straw man outline and the group discussions. Most of the volunteers had little experience or training with CM. Accordingly, volunteers were assigned where their other experiences would prove beneficial. The volunteers with CM experience were assigned as leads for particular sections of the practice standard.

The guiding principles for the Practice Standard on Project Configuration Management:
- Provides guidelines that are relevant to project managers and project teams on the requirements and responsibilities of a sound CM system for their project;
- Is consistent with the *PMBOK® Guide*–Third Edition;
- Does not mirror the *PMBOK® Guide*–Third Edition, but provides additional background and detailed information on the practice of configuration management and is more prescriptive than the *PMBOK® Guide*–Third Edition;
- Aligns itself with other PMI, American, and International standards, as well as common practices within the field. Future editions will continue to refresh the material and keep the practice standard aligned with future practices implemented by the leaders within the field;
- Provides the *what, when,* and *why* CM should be implemented on projects; and
- Contains templates and samples of templates and structures used for a successful CM process. Detailed information shall be provided on the use of each of the samples and templates.

Appendix C

Contributors and Reviewers of the Practice Standard on Project Configuration Management

C.1 PSPCM Project Leadership Team

The following individuals served as members, were contributors of text or concepts, and served as leaders within the Project Leadership Team (PLT).

Elden F. Jones II, MSPM, PMP	**Project Manager**
Lynn M. Connolly	**Deputy Project Manager**
Terry R. Anderson, PMP	**Content Manager**
Ganesh Virupakshan	**Configuration Manager**
Fabio Salazar, PMP	**Quality Assurance**
Herman Gonzalez, PMP	**Quality Control**
Kackie Cohen	**Editing Manager**

C.2 PSPCM Project Core Team

In addition to the PLT, the following individuals served as members, were contributors of text or concepts, and served as members or leaders within the Project Core Team (PLT).

Erin Velie, PMP (Lead)	**Front/Back Matter**
Carol A. Long, CEng, SMIEEE	
Harshavardhan Chakravarti, B.S.	
John Machado, PE (Lead)	**CM Management & Planning**
Richard E. Beihl, CSQE, CSSBB	
Amitabh Choudhary, PMP	
Garrett L. Pope, PMP	
Don Cole, PMP (Lead)	**Configuration Identification**
Karen Rasmussen Noll	
Shivlal Yadav, PMP (Lead)	**Configuration Change Management**
David Hughes, PMP	

Susan Strople, PMP (Lead)	**Configuration Status Accounting &**
Job A.Vazquez, PhD	**Metrics**
George Jackelen, PMP (Lead)	**Configuration Verification & Audits**
Bernagail Wilcox, CSM	
Vladimir Antonio Mininel, PMP	
Mahender Narala, PMP	**Internal Review**
Marcia Carrere	

C.3 Additional Team Members

The following members of the team provided review comments, content information, or other facets as being a part of the *Practice Standard on Project Configuration Management* team:

Warija Adiga, PMP	David S. Guzunsky, CCS
Baris Akkaya, PMP	Sabastien Hadjifotis
Abdullah Ali Al-Harbi	Pramila Hari, PMP
Cristiano L. Alkaim, PMP	ING. Pedro Helguero, PMP
Selim Alkaner, PhD, PMP	Amanda Hope
Saranet T. Annamalai, PMP	Gail A. Howe
Sreenivas Atluri, PMP	Patricia L. Hubbard
David Bandelli	Isao Indo, PMP
Sapna Bhargava	Srinivas Iyengar B'Com, A.C.A.
Jerzy Bielonko, PMP	Naseem Jadavji
Michael F. Blankenstein, MS, PMP	Catherine Jaggard, PhD
Praveen Kumar Bojja, MBA, PMP	M. Aamir Jelani
Dr. David Bonyuet, PMP	Shimalatha Joseph
Rollin O. Bowen Jr.	Harry L. Kendrick
Stephen Bragner	Darrell L. Jorgensen, PMP
Ketty Brown, PMP	Mallikarjuna R. Kesavaraju, PMP
Adrian Busch, PMP, MBA	Manoj Khanna
John E. Canepari	Atchutarao Killamsetty, PMP
Sangeeta Carter	Michael R. Kinzly, PMP
Henrique G. Castro, PMP	Agnieszka Kosicka, PMP
Nalinee Chinowuthichai	Monica Kour
Veronica Cooperman	Brahama James Kroma
Chamroeum Dee, BS	Kumar Praveen Mysore
Angelia D. Dinkins	Revendra Kumar, PMP
Calum Downie, PMP	Sai Kiran Kumar
Sweeton S. Ebiraj, PMP	Suresh Kumar Tangella
Judy Edwards, PhD, PMP	Arthur LeRoy Lawrence
Dora Erasmo	Raymond C. Lui
Anna Maria Felici, PMP	Anoop Madhavan, PMP, CQA
John Wayne Fischer Jr.	Paulraj Manickam
Fabio G. Frias	Shayan R. Mashatian
Venkatadurga Nageshbabu Garapati, PMP	Sudhir B. Menon
Santosh Lawoo Gawande	Darrien R. Michael
Syamak Ghorashi, PMP	Jorge S. Miranda Cruz
John Glander	Vicki L. Mitchell
Monique E. Goodman	John N. Morfaw, MBA, PMP

Robert A. Moylan, MCSE
Jonathan S. Myerov
Joan N. Neufeld, PMP
Leonard Ong, PMP, CISSP
Dhruv Ranchhoddas Parekh, PMP
Patrick Pearce
Stephen F. Randolph, PMBA, PMP
Arthur Richard, PMP, CISA
Alberto Riveros
Daniel J. Rosati, PMP
Mario Salmona Petersen, PE, PMP
Steve Smith, PMP
Vineet Sood, P.Eng, PMP
Renuka K. Srinivasan, PMP
Eric Sugar

Paraminder S. Talwar, PMP
Chirag B. Thaker, PMP
Alex Thomas
George Velimachitis
Irina V. Vladimirov
Vilim W. Vranovic
Sergei Vratenkov
Len White, PMP
Gwen Whitman, PMP
Douglas K. Williams, PMP
Marsha E. Williams
Lai-chi Wong, PMP
Seung Bum Yang, PMP
Paul Yates

C.4 Final Exposure Draft Reviewers and Contributors

In addition to team members, the following individuals provided recommendations for improving the Exposure Draft of the *Practice Standard on Project Configuration Management:*

Hussain Ali Al-Ansari, Eur Ing, CEng
Mohammed Abdulla Al-Kuwari, PMP, CEng
Mohammed Safi Batley, MIM
Michael J. L. Day, P. Eng.
Dorothy L. Kangas, PMP, SCPM
Kazuhiko Okubo, PE, PMP
Crispin ("Kik") Piney, BSc, PMP
Margaret H. M. Schaeken, B.Sc.(Math), PMP
Carol Steuer, PMP
Patrick Weaver, PMP, FAICD
Rebecca A. Winston, JD

C.5 PMI Project Management Standards Program Member Advisory Group

The following individuals served as members of the PMI Standards Program Member Advisory Group during development of the *Practice Standard on Project Configuration Management*:

Julia M. Bednar, PMP
Sergio R. Coronado
J. Brian Hobbs, PMP
Carol Holliday, PMP
Thomas Kurihara
Debbie O'Bray
Asbjorn Rolstadas, PhD
Cyndi Stackpole, PMP
Bobbye Underwood, PMP
Dave Violette, MPM, PMP

C.6 Production Staff

Special mention is due to the following employees of PMI:

Ruth Anne Guerrero, MBA, PMP–Standards Manager

Dottie Nichols, PMP–Standards Manager

Kristin L. Vitello–Standards Project Specialist

Nan Wolfslayer–Standards Project Specialist

Barbara Walsh–Publications Planner

Roberta Storer–Product Editor

Dan Goldfischer–Editor-in-Chief

Appendix D

Examples and Additional Configuration Management (CM) Information

A number of examples are available on the World Wide Web. These examples range from the very general to those with considerable detail.

- A template for documentation can be found at http://www.rcglobal.com/wrcglsept27rgsamp.htm
- The process used by the U.S. Department of Defense is described in MIL-HDBK-61A, http://www.acq.osd.mil/io/se/Old%20Files/cm&dm/pdf_files/MIL-HDBK-61A.pdf
- For software projects, the Software Engineering Institute (SEI) at Carnegie-Mellon University provides a high-level process that could be adopted for project CM. Refer to http://www.sei.cmu.edu/cmmi/background/ccb-process-flow.pdf
- Processes used by the State of California are available at http://www.bestpractices.cahwnet.gov/downloads/BP%20Website%20Topic%20-%20change%20control%203242_2.PDF
  A fresh new look at configuration management and its evolution is found at http://www.icmhq.com as an example in Figure E-1.
- The Prince system is found at http://www.ogc.gov.uk/prince

Appendix E

Sample Configuration Management (CM) Processes and Forms

E.1 Sample Process

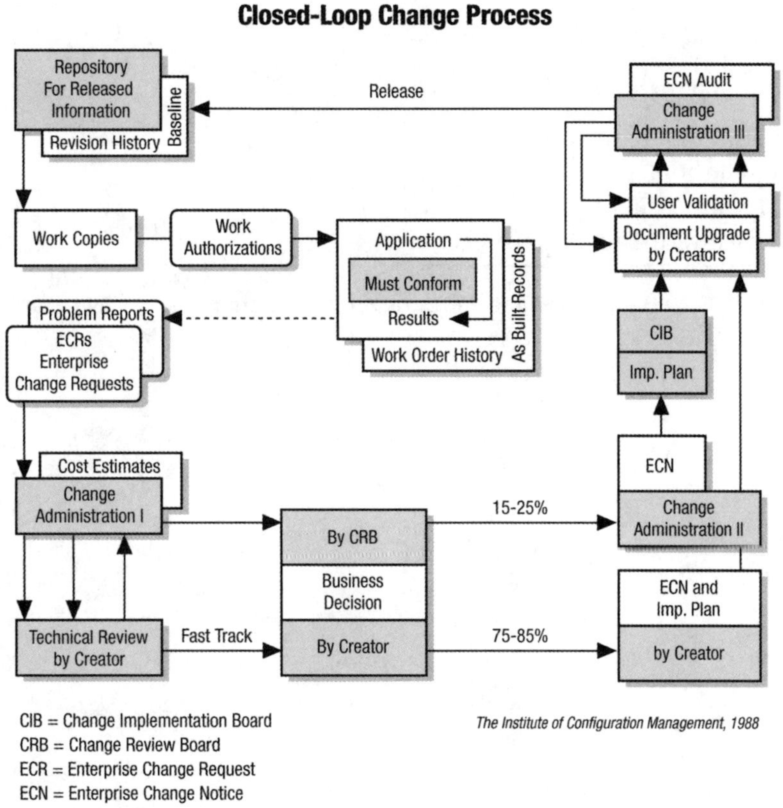

Closed-Loop Change Process

CIB = Change Implementation Board
CRB = Change Review Board
ECR = Enterprise Change Request
ECN = Enterprise Change Notice

The Institute of Configuration Management, 1988

Figure E-1. Exhibit Closed Loop Process from the Institute of Configuration Management

E.2 Sample CM Plan Outline

1. Introduction
2. Scope
   2.1 Configuration Items (CIs)
   2.2 Other Items Included Under the Project Configuration Management (PCM) Plan
   2.3 Applicability of PCM
   2.4 Limitations That Apply To the PCM Plan
   2.5 Assumptions
   2.6 Key Terms
   2.7 References
3. PCM
   3.1 Organization
   3.2 PCM Responsibilities
   3.3 Applicable Policies, Directives, and Procedures
   3.4 Tools and Infrastructure
4. PCM Activities
   4.1 Configuration Identification
   4.2 Configuration Control
   4.3 Configuration Status Accounting
   4.4 Configuration Audits and Reviews
   4.5 Interface Control
   4.6 Subcontractor/Vendor Control
5. PCM Schedule
6. PCM Resources
7. PCM Plan Maintenance
8. PCM Tailoring
   8.1 Upward Tailoring
   8.2 Downward Tailoring

Figure E-2. Sample Outline for Configuration Management (CM) Plan

E.3 Change Control Forms

E.3.1 Example 1:

The PRINCE system uses the following Configuration Item Record template for Configuration Change Control:

CONFIGURATION ITEM RECORD				
Project name				
Release	Draft/Final Date:			
PRINCE2				
Author:				
Owner:				
Client:				
Document Number:				
DOCUMENT HISTORY				
Document Location				
Revision History				
Revision Date	Previous Revision Date	Summary of Changes		Changes marked
Approvals				
Name	Signature	Title	Date of Issue	Version
Distribution				
Name	Title	Date of Issue	Version	

Figure E-3. Change Control Form—Example 1 (*continued*)

PURPOSE	
Contents	
Project Identifier	
Type of Deliverable	
Deliverable Identifier	
Latest Version Number	
Deliverable Description	
Description of the Life Cycle Steps Appropriate to the Deliverable	
Owner of the Deliverable	
Person Working on the Deliverable	
Date Allocated	
Library or Location Where the Deliverable is Kept	
Source	
Links to Related Deliverables	
Status	
Copy Holders or Potential Users	
Cross Reference— Project Issues	
Cross Reference— Correspondence	

©Crown Copyright

Figure E-3. Change Control Form—Example 1

E3.2 Example 2:

Control Number

Section 1 Tracking Information **(Submitter Complete)**

Originator		Sponsor	
Phone		Phone	
Location		Location	
Source		Authority	
Date		Need Date	
Why that Need Date?			

Title

Description

Section 2 Brief Analysis **(Technical Lead)**

Impact

Check All that Apply

Classification
- ☐ Facility
- ☐ Hardware
- ☐ Software
- ☐ Documentation

Priority
- ☐ Emergency
- ☐ Urgent
- ☐ High
- ☐ Medium
- ☐ Low

Severity
- ☐ Catastrophic
- ☐ Major
- ☐ Minor
- ☐ Cosmetic
- ☐ Enhancement

Cost
- ☐ 0 - $24,999
- ☐ $25K - $49,999
- ☐ $50K - $89,999
- ☐ $90K - $99,999
- ☐ Over $100K

Level of Effort
- ☐ < 1 Man Month
- ☐ 1 - 3 Man Months
- ☐ 4 - 6 Man Months
- ☐ 7 - 12 Man Months
- ☐ Over 12 Man Months

Feasibility

Technical	☐ Yes	☐ No
Legal	☐ Yes	☐ No
Functional	☐ Yes	☐ No

Section 3 Technical Review Board Disposition

☐ Approved ☐ Disapproved ☐ Fast Track

☐ Deferred Until ____________ Chair ____________

☐ Analysis Lead Assigned Date ____________

Analysis Lead ____________ Due Date ____________

Figure E-4. Change Control Form—Example 2 (*continued*)

Section 4 Detailed Analysis Summary   **(Supporting documentation required)**

Impact

[_____]

Documents
Impacted

[_____]

Check All
that Apply

Classification	**Priority**	**Severity**
☐ Facility	☐ Emergency	☐ Catastrophic
☐ Hardware	☐ Urgent	☐ Major
☐ Software	☐ High	☐ Minor
☐ Documentation	☐ Medium	☐ Cosmetic
	☐ Low	☐ Enhancement

Cost	**Level of Effort**	**Feasibility**		
☐ 0 - $24,999	☐ < 1 Man Month	Technical	☐ Yes	☐ No
☐ $25K - $49,999	☐ 1 - 3 Man Months	Legal	☐ Yes	☐ No
☐ $50K - $89,999	☐ 4 - 6 Man Months	Functional	☐ Yes	☐ No
☐ $90K - $99,999	☐ 7 - 12 Man Months			
☐ Over $100K	☐ Over 12 Man Months			

Risk Factor (1-10) [_____]   Low = 1   **Opportunity Factor** (1-10) [_____]

Section 5 Change Review Board Disposition

☐ Approve for Implementation on _____   ☐ Fast Track
☐ Deferred Until _____   Chair _____
☐ Disapproved   Date _____

Section 5 Change Implementation Board Disposition

☐ Approve for Implementation on _____   ☐ Fast Track
☐ Deferred Until _____   Chair _____
☐ Disapproved   Date _____

Figure E-4. Change Control Form—Example 2 (*continued*)

Classification

Facility - Any change in the make-up of facilities (non-IT) which affects the Project.
Hardware - Any change to an IT hardware item.
Software - Any change to an IT software item.
Documentation - Any change of documentation that does not affect IT configuration.

Priority

Emergency - Any items that must be implemented before the next business day.
Urgent - Severe usability problems for external users.
High - Severe usability problems for internal users.
Medium - No severe impact, but rectification cannot be deferred until next release.
Low - Change is justified, but can wait upon release schedule.

Severity

Catastrophic - Problem is critical to project development and stops work in major area.
Major - Problem has an unacceptable impact on the project development even with a work around.
Minor - Problem can be circumvented in an acceptable way.
Cosmetic - Problem does not materially impact on the project development.
Enhancement - Item that is not currently in the design, however would contribute to the system.

Disposition

Approved - Enough analysis is presented in order to recommend progression into the next step of development.
Deferred - More analysis is required before a decision can be achieved.
Disapproved - From the analysis performed, it is deemed that this change is not feasible.
Analysis Lead Assigned - Brief analysis indicates that an in-depth analysis is warranted. An analysis lead is assigned with the leader announced.

Figure E-4. Change Control Form—Example 2

Appendix F

Additional Sources of Information on Configuration Management

A list of documents and standards that may be applicable to configuration management:

[1] DoD 5200.22-M, National Industrial Security Program Operating Manual (NISPOM)

[2] DoD-STD-2168, Defense System Software Quality Program

[3] EIA/IEEE 632, Processes for Engineering a System

[4] EIA/IEEE 649, National Consensus Standard for Configuration Management

[5] EIA/IEEE 12207, Software Development

[6] FAA Standard 8100.7, Aircraft Certification Systems Evaluation Program

[7] FIPS PUB 152, Standard Generalized Markup Language (SGML)

[8] ISO 9000 (Series), Quality Systems

[9] MIL-HDBK-61, Configuration Management Guidance

[10] MIL-STD-498, Defense Systems Software Management

[11] MIL-STD-881, Work Breakdown Structure

[12] SEI-93-TR-24, Capability Maturity Model for Software

[13] Basic Principals of Practical Configuration Management eLearning by Systems and Software Productivity Consortium [www.software.org]

[14] Horn, Steve, "Deming's System of Profound Knowledge," [http://home.clara.net/hornsc/spk/spk_intro.htm]

[15] Institute of Configuration Management (ICM) White Paper, "Project Management Relative to CMII," Web source: [http://www.icmhq.com/CMII%20White%20Papers/Project_Mgmt.pdf]

[16] Kasse, T., McQuaid, P. A., Kasse Initatives, LLC, and California Polytechnic University, "Software Configuration Management for Project Leaders," The American Society for Quality (ASQ) publications: Software Quality Professional: Volume 2, Issue 4, September 2000. Web source: [http://www.asq.org/pub/sqp/past/vol2 issue4/mcquaid.html]

[17] Morris, PWG, "Science, Objective Knowledge and the Theory of Project Management,"*P I CIVIL ENG-CIV EN*, Vol 150, No. 2, pp 82-90, May 2002

Glossary

1. Definitions

Many of the words defined here have broader, and in some cases, different dictionary definitions. The definitions use the following conventions:

- Terms used as part of the definitions and that are defined in the glossary are shown in *italics.*
  - When the same glossary term appears more than once in a given definition, only the first occurrence is italicized.
  - In some cases, a single glossary term consists of multiple words (e.g., configuration management planning).
  - In many cases, there are multiple, consecutive glossary terms within a given definition. For example, *duration estimate* denotes two separate glossary entries, one for "duration" and another for "estimate." (There are even some definitions with a string of consecutive italicized words, not separated by commas that represent multiple, consecutive glossary terms at least one of which consists of multiple words. For example, *critical path method late finish date* denotes two separate glossary entries, one for "critical path method" and another for "late finish date.")
- When synonyms are included, no definition is given and the reader is directed to the preferred term (i.e., see preferred term).
- Related terms that are not synonyms are cross-referenced at the end of the definition (i.e., see also related term).

Accept. The act of formally receiving or acknowledging something and regarding it as being true, sound, suitable, or complete. (*PMBOK® Guide*–Third Edition)

Acceptance. SEE Accept

Activity. A component of work performed during the course of a project. (*PMBOK® Guide*–Third Edition)

Approval. SEE Approve

Approve. The act of formally confirming, sanctioning, ratifying, or agreeing to something. (*PMBOK® Guide*–Third Edition)

Artifact. Information that is both concrete and tangible, such as a document or electronic file. Processes are applied to artifacts to enable creation, modification, and control. Often artifacts are relevant to phases in the project life cycle, such as a schedule during the planning phase or a risk analysis during the execution of a project.

Audit. A planned and documented *activity* performed by qualified personnel to determine by investigation, examination, or evaluation of objective evidence, the adequacy and compliance with established procedures or applicable documents and the effectiveness of implementation.

Baseline. The *approved* time phased plan (for a project, a work breakdown structure component, a work package, or a schedule *activity*), plus or minus approved project scope, cost, schedule, and technical *changes*. Generally refers to the current baseline, but may refer to the original or some other baseline. Usually used with a modifier (e.g., cost baseline, schedule baseline, performance measurement baseline, technical baseline). (*PMBOK® Guide*–Third Edition)

Bug. SEE Problem.

Change. Any occurrence of deviation from expected outcomes, where the deliverable is performing to specifications and the specifications are in error.

Change Control. Identifying, documenting, approving or rejecting, and controlling *changes* to the project *baselines*. (*PMBOK® Guide*–Third Edition)

Change Control Board (CCB). A formally constituted group of *stakeholders* responsible for reviewing, evaluating, approving, delaying, or rejecting *changes* to the project, with all decisions and recommendations being recorded. (*PMBOK® Guide*–Third Edition)

Change History. A description of how and why a revision of a *configuration item* differs from its prior *version*.

Change Implementation Board. A formally constituted group of *stakeholders* responsible for reviewing, evaluating, approving, delaying, or rejecting *changes* to the project based on implementation reasons such as schedule or cost.

Change Notice. A grouping of *change requests*. Groupings are normally based on like *changes* or changes to the same area of the project's deliverables.

Change Review Board. A formally constituted group of *stakeholders* responsible for reviewing, evaluating, approving, delaying, or rejecting *changes* to the project based on business reasons such as strategic focus or business implementation plans.

Change Request. Requests to expand or reduce the project scope, modify policies, processes, plans, or procedures, modify costs or budgets, or revise schedules. Requests for a *change* can be direct or indirect, externally or internally initiated, and legally or contractually mandated or optional. Only formally documented requested changes are processed and only *approved* change requests are implemented. (*PMBOK® Guide*–Third Edition)

Configuration. Physical and functional arrangement of interconnected parts that form a system, a piece of equipment or a product. [Paraphrased ISO 10007].

Configuration Change Management. Ensures *(1)* regulation of the flow of proposed *changes*, *(2)* documentation of the complete impact of the proposed changes, and *(3) release* only of *approved configuration* changes into project products and their related configuration documentation. SEE Integrated Change Control.

Configuration Control. The application of agreed upon rules in order to ensure that all modifications to *configuration items* are submitted and analyzed prior to providing a disposition and that all such requests and *changes* are recorded in a traceable manner.

Configuration Control Board (CCB). SEE Change Control Board.

Configuration Identification. Selection of *configuration items*, and identification of their functional and physical characteristics. This provides the basis from which the *configuration* of deliverables is defined and verified, products and *artifacts* are labeled, *changes* are managed, and accountability is maintained.

Configuration Item. Aggregation of hardware, software, processed materials, services, or any of its discrete portions, which satisfy an end-use function, and whose requirements are specific and designated for separate *configuration management*. [Paraphrased ISO 10007].

Configuration Management (CM). Management process to establish and maintain consistency of a product's performance, functional and physical attributes with its requirements, design, and operational information throughout its life [EIA-649].

Configuration Management Control. SEE Configuration Control.

Configuration Management Harmonization. Describes a condition where the *configuration management* system on a project manages unique *configuration items* in a way to ensure they do not conflict in practice, schedule, or resource usage; and where they share a common vocabulary needed for effective communications among *stakeholders*.

Configuration Management Plan. *Configuration* planning which outlines the overall processes and procedures to be employed for *configuration management*. Describes what (not how) configuration management must accomplish and what consistency must remain between the deliverable definition, deliverable configuration, and configuration management records throughout all phases of the project life cycle.

Configuration Management Planning. The development and planning of *configuration management* processes for the context and environment in which they are to be performed.

Configuration Status Accounting. An element of *configuration management* that consists of the recording and reporting of information needed to effectively manage a *configuration item*. This information includes a listing of *approved configuration identification*, status of proposed *changes* to *configuration*, and the implementation status of approved changes.

Configuration Verification and Audit. The process of ensuring the result of a *configuration item* meets pre-defined criteria (requirements). Establishes that the performance and functional requirements defined in the *configuration* documentation have been achieved by the design and that the design has been accurately documented in the configuration documentation.

Effectivity. Specification of the point at which a *change* will be effective. The effectivity is based upon the type of deliverable being addressed and is associated with either a date, a build, a *release*, a lot, or a serial number classification. (e.g. "effective date").

Enhancement Any condition where a *stakeholder* (customer, user, developer, etc.) finds an area that may be enhanced or improved.

Enterprise Configuration Management Plan. *Configuration* planning which outlines the overall processes and procedures to be employed for *configuration management* at an organization or portfolio level.

Functional Configuration Audit. An *audit* conducted to verify that the development of a *configuration item* has been completed satisfactorily; that it is operational or useable; and that the support documents are complete and satisfactory.

Integrated Change Control [Process]. The process of reviewing all *change requests*, approving *changes* and controlling changes to deliverables and organizational process assets. (*PMBOK® Guide*–Third Edition)

Item. See Configuration Item.

Physical Configuration Audit. An *audit* conducted to verify that a *configuration item* (or group of configuration items) matches documented descriptions and requirements.

Problem. Any occurrence of deviation from expected outcomes, where the deliverable is not performing to defined specifications.

Project Artifact. See Artifact.

Project Configuration Management. A subset of project management that comprises the collective body of processes, activities, tools, and methods used to manage designated project deliverables or *artifacts* throughout the project life cycle. It consists of *configuration management planning*, *configuration identification*, *configuration change management*, *configuration status accounting*, and *configuration verification and audits*.

Project Configuration Management Plan. A project configuration management plan is a subsidiary of the project management plan. It can also be a subset of the *enterprise configuration management plan*, and will use the enterprise plan as a guideline to ensure compliance and integration with an organization's overall plans.

Release. An action whereby a particular *version* of a *configuration item* or group of configuration items is made available.

Stakeholder. Person or organization (e.g., customer, sponsor, performing organization, or the public) that is actively involved in the project, or whose interests may be positively or negatively affected by execution or completion of the project. A stakeholder may also exert influence over the project and its deliverables. (*PMBOK® Guide*–Third Edition)

Technical Review Board. A formally or informally constituted group of subject matter experts within the project responsible for reviewing, evaluating, approving, delaying, or rejecting *changes* to the project based on technical reasons such as capabilities and functionality.

Verification [Technique]. The technique of evaluating a component or product at the end of a phase or project to assure or confirm it satisfies the conditions imposed. (*PMBOK® Guide*–Third Edition)

Version. A uniquely identified instance of a *configuration item*.

Version Control. A means to identify and manage *configuration items* as they change over time.

2. Acronyms

ASME	American Society of Mechanical Engineers
CCB	Configuration or change control board
CCM	Configuration change management
CI	Configuration item
CM	Configuration management
CMP	Configuration management plan
CR	Change request
ECN	Enterprise change notice
ECR	Enterprise change request
EIA	Electronic Industries Alliance
FCA	Functional configuration audit
FMEA	Failure mode and effect analysis
ID	Identification
IEEE	Institute of Electrical and Electronic Engineers
ISO	International Organization for Standardization
OPM3®	Organizational Project Management Maturity Model
PCA	Physical configuration audit
PCM	Project configuration management
PMBOK® Guide	*A Guide to the Project Management Body of Knowledge*
PMI	Project Management Institute
PMIS	Project management information system
PSPCM	*Practice Standard on Configuration Management*
SPC	Statistical process control
WBS	Work breakdown structure

Index by Keyword